AF598970

TELEPHONES
THEN AND NOW

CYNTHIA KENNEDY HENZEL

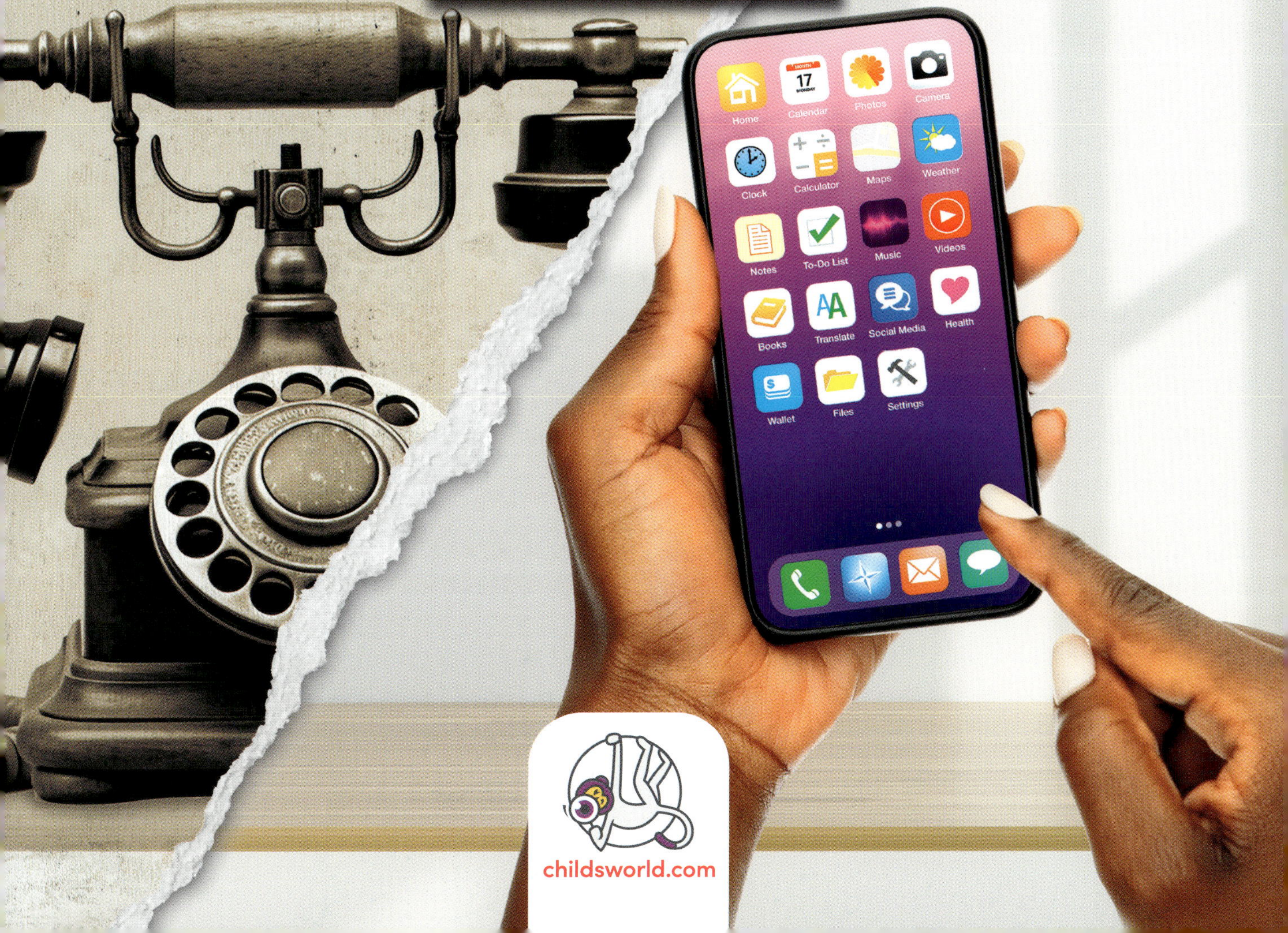

childsworld.com

Published by The Child's World®
800-599-READ · www.childsworld.com

Photography Credits
Photographs ©: Shutterstock Images, cover (background), cover (old phone), 1 (background), 1 (old phone), 3 (background), 4–5, 9, 12–13, 14, 18, 20, 22; Ground Picture/ Shutterstock Images, cover (modern phone), 1 (modern phone); Kaspars Grinvalds/Shutterstock Images, cover (phone screen), 1 (phone screen); Molas Images/ Shutterstock Images, cover (icon), 1 (icon), 3 (icon), 4; Harris & Ewing/Library of Congress, 7; Everett Collection/ Shutterstock Images, 10–11; Red Line Editorial, 17

ISBN Information
9781503889521 (Reinforced Library Binding)
9781503891142 (Portable Document Format)
9781503892385 (Online Multi-user eBook)
9781503893627 (Electronic Publication)

LCCN 2023950244

Printed in the United States of America

Cynthia Kennedy Henzel has a BS in social studies education and an MS in geography. She has worked as a teacher-educator in many countries. Currently, she writes fiction and nonfiction books and develops educational materials for social studies, history, science, and ELL students. She has written more than 100 books and 150 stories for young people.

TABLE OF CONTENTS

TELEPHONES

Telephones have been around since the late 1800s. Since then, they have become an important part of daily life. The average American spends more than 4.5 hours on their phone every day. Phones make it easy to talk to friends and family. Businesses use telephones to reach customers. People use phones to find information. They shop on their phones. They even use them to count how many steps they take. But people can spend too much time on phones. Phones may keep people from doing other things, such as going out with friends, exercising, or reading books.

In 2023, Americans checked their phones every 10 minutes on average.

CALL THE OPERATOR

In the mid-1800s, some people searched for ways to send sound **electronically**. One of these people was inventor Alexander Graham Bell. In 1876, Bell received a **patent** for the telephone. By 1878, his first customers were calling one another. At the time, each telephone had a wire that went to a central office. These wires were called landlines. The wires were connected to a large board with holes in it. This was called a switchboard.

To make a call, the caller lifted the telephone's **receiver** from a hook. This powered up the telephone. A telephone operator at the switchboard answered.

Alexander Graham Bell was born in Scotland in 1847. He moved to the United States in 1871.

The caller asked to talk to another person who had a telephone on the switchboard. The operator connected the wires on the switchboard between the two telephones. The second telephone rang. Someone picked up the receiver. Then the people could talk.

In 1879, companies began giving each telephone a number. This made them easier to remember. In 1891, inventor Almon Strowger invented a way to make a call without an operator. He put a **dial** on the telephone. The dial had ten holes. Each hole was next to a number from 0 to 9. Each number was associated with a few letters. For example, 2 was usually associated with the letters A, B, and C. People put their finger into the hole next to the number or letter they wanted. Then they turned the dial. This way, people could call specific phone numbers.

At first, people could dial only local calls. They still called the operator to speak with someone far away. This was expensive. In 1920, a 10-minute call from California to New York cost $26.17. That would be more than $400 in 2023.

PAYPHONES

People without phones at home could use a payphone. This was a telephone in a public place. People put coins into the payphone to make a call. Payphones became common in the early 1900s.

Early telephone numbers also had letters.

CHAPTER 2

WIRELESS PHONES

By 1945, there was a telephone for every five people in the United States. Alexander Graham Bell's company had become AT&T. It owned the switchboards and telephone lines. It even owned the telephones in people's homes. People rented them from the telephone company.

Telephones were changing the world. Businesses could get things done faster. People could get emergency help quickly.

Telephone operators mostly disappeared by the 1980s.

The 911 emergency line first opened in parts of the United States in 1968.

911
EMERGENCY CALL

People from different countries could talk to each other, too. This brought the world closer together. Some people worried about the bad effects of telephones. They were concerned that people would forget how to write letters.

Sometimes telephone calls were not **private**. Operators could listen to people talking. To save money, many homes shared a telephone line with other homes. This was called a party line. Each home had a special ring. This let people know which home the call was for. But anyone on the party line could pick up their phone and listen to other people talk.

Early cell phones sent and received signals using a long piece of metal called an antenna.

In 1973, new technology changed the telephone system. Engineer Martin Cooper made the first cell-phone call. Cell phones worked by sending signals through the air to cell towers. There were no wires.

In 1983, a cell phone cost $3,500. That would be $10,600 in 2023. It was the size of a brick and weighed 2.5 pounds (1.1 kg).

The phone took 10 hours to charge. A person could talk for 35 minutes on a full charge. But technology improved quickly. Prices went down. By 1990, 1 million Americans had a cell phone. And people could do more than talk. They could send text messages. In 1997, the company Nokia released an early mobile game. It was called *Snake*.

Technology was about to change again. New devices called smartphones combined a cell phone with a portable computer. The first smartphone came out in 1992. Then, in 2007, Apple introduced the first iPhone. It was very popular. Users could make calls, listen to music, browse the web, and more. By 2011, 35 percent of Americans owned smartphones.

AN APP FOR THAT

By 2023, 85 percent of Americans had smartphones. Now, people around the world communicate in many ways on smartphones. They send pictures or talk on video calls. They send text messages and emails. People also communicate on social media networks. These are online services where people can talk and share interests. Social media **applications**, or apps, such as Facebook and TikTok have billions of users.

WORLDWIDE SMARTPHONE SALES BY YEAR

Smartphone sales went down in 2020 for many reasons. One of them is that lots of people kept their old phones for longer.

SMARTPHONE WASTE

Americans throw away millions of smartphones each year. Smartphone waste contributes to pollution. People can help by keeping their phones longer and recycling old phones.

People can play smartphone games with others using the internet.

Smartphones provide information. Students search the internet for school reports. People get news from websites, apps, and **podcasts**. Travelers can access maps and directions. People also use their smartphones to shop. They buy items online or make payments in stores. They pay bills. They send money to friends.

Smartphones are also used for entertainment. People listen to music. They play games. They watch videos. There are millions of apps. There is an app for almost everything. Some help people stay healthy. Others help people learn new languages.

Phones have some downsides, too. Using phones instead of meeting with other people in person can make people lonelier. People can use smartphones to spread harmful information about others. Private information put online can be stolen. Learning to protect privacy is an important skill for smartphone users.

Phones of the future may be able to make holograms, which are 3D images made of light.

Telephone technology is still changing. Someday, phones might be able to display 3D pictures. New apps might be able to tell if people are sick. Phones have come a long way since they were first invented. And there is a lot to look forward to in the future.

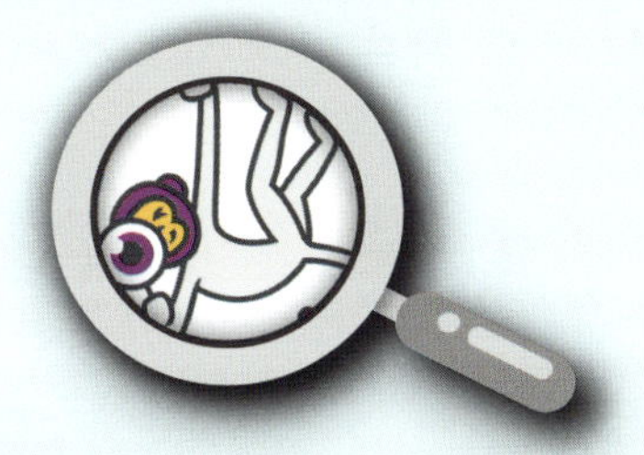

WONDER MORE

Wondering about New Information

How much did you know about early telephones before reading this book? What information did you learn? Write down three new facts that this book taught you. Was the information surprising? Why or why not?

Wondering How It Matters

What is one way telephones relate to your life? If you cannot think of a personal connection, imagine a way telephones might affect other kids. What impact might phones have on their lives?

Wondering Why

People use smartphones for everyday tasks. Smartphones can save people time. But they also come with problems. Do you think depending on smartphones is a good thing? Why or why not?

Ways to Keep Wondering

Getting information from a smartphone is easy. But not all information people find is true. What can you do to find out whether the information you find online can be trusted?

FAST FACTS

- Alexander Graham Bell received a patent for the telephone in 1876.
- Early telephones were wired together by landlines.
- Telephone operators connected wires on a switchboard to connect calls.
- Dial phones allowed people to connect calls themselves.
- Cell phones send signals through the air instead of over telephone lines.
- Cell phones allow people to talk, write messages, and play games on their phones.
- Smartphones combine cell phones with computers.
- Smartphones allow people to connect to the internet on their phones.
- Apps on smartphones let people build communities, listen to music, find information, and do lots of other things.
- It is important for smartphone users to protect their privacy online.

GLOSSARY

applications (ap-luh-KAY-shuhnz) Applications are software on smartphones that do particular tasks. Social media applications are used by people around the world.

dial (DYE-uhl) A dial is a flat, round plate that can be turned to different numbers. Some telephones have a dial.

electronically (ee-lek-TRAH-nik-lee) A device works electronically if it is powered by electricity. Telephones send sound electronically.

patent (PAT-int) A patent is a right given by a government to keep others from making or selling a new invention. Alexander Graham Bell received a patent for the telephone.

podcasts (POD-kastz) Podcasts are audio files containing programs similar to radio broadcasts. People can listen to podcasts on smartphones.

pollution (puh-LOO-shuhn) Pollution is something harmful added to the environment. Throwing away smartphones can add to pollution.

private (PRY-vit) Private information belongs only to a specific person or group. Smartphone users need to protect their private information.

receiver (ruh-SEE-vur) The receiver is the part of the telephone where electrical signals become sound. With some telephones, users must hold the receiver near their ear.

FIND OUT MORE

In the Library

Higgins, Nadia. *How Do Cell Phones Work?* Parker, CO: The Child's World, 2022.

Keppeler, Jill. *20 Fun Facts About the Telephone.* New York, NY: Gareth Stevens, 2024.

Proudfit, Benjamin. *Alexander Graham Bell and the Telephone.* New York, NY: Gareth Stevens, 2023.

On the Web

Visit our website for links about telephones:
childsworld.com/links

Note to Parents, Caregivers, Teachers, and Librarians: We routinely verify our web links to make sure they are safe and active sites. So encourage your readers to check them out!

INDEX